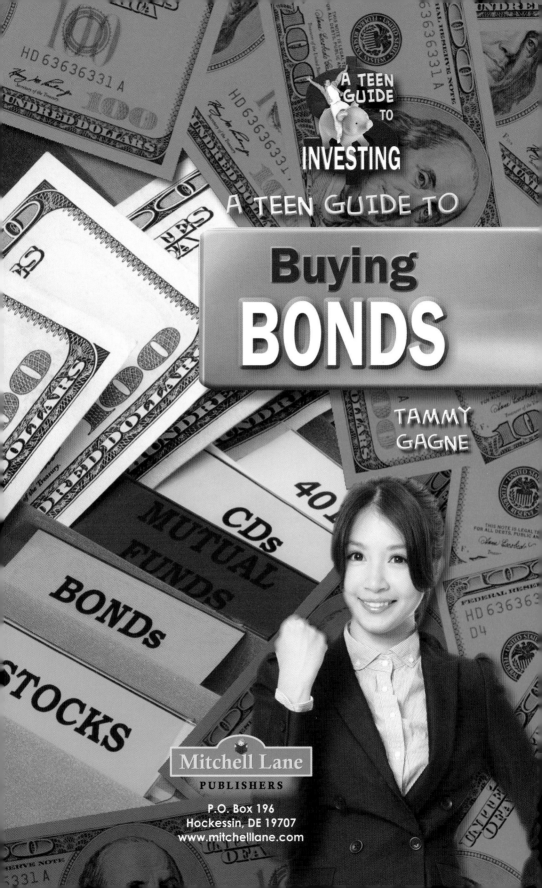

A TEEN GUIDE TO INVESTING

A TEEN GUIDE TO

Buying
BONDS

TAMMY GAGNE

Mitchell Lane
PUBLISHERS

P.O. Box 196
Hockessin, DE 19707
www.mitchelllane.com

A TEEN GUIDE TO INVESTING

Investment Options for Teens
A Teen Guide to Buying Stocks
A Dividend Stock Strategy for Teens
A Teen Guide to Buying Bonds
A Teen Guide to Buying Mutual Funds
A Teen Guide to Safe-Haven Savings

Printing   1   2   3   4   5   6   7   8   9

Library of Congress
Cataloging-in-Publication Data
Gagne, Tammy.
 A teen guide to buying bonds / by Tammy Gagne.
    pages cm. — (A teen guide to investing)
  Includes bibliographical references and index.
  Audience: Grade 7 to 8.
  ISBN 978-1-61228-424-8 (library bound)
  1. Bonds—Juvenile literature. 2. Investments—Juvenile literature. 3. Finance, Personal—Juvenile literature. I. Title.
  HG4651.G34 2014
  332.63'23—dc23
                                              2013014379

eBook ISBN: 9781612284866

PLB

Contents

Loaning money to
the government or
big businesses can
really pay off.

CHAPTER 1

The Beginning of BONDS

Sooner or later almost everyone needs to borrow money. Perhaps you have asked your parents to loan you money until you got your allowance so you could go to the movies with a friend. When you get older, you may need to borrow money from a bank to buy your first car. Chances are good that your parents had to borrow money to buy their home. Just like people, businesses and governments also need to borrow money sometimes.

A bond is a loan that an investor makes to either a private company or the government. You may also hear people refer to bonds as debt securities. Both corporations and Uncle Sam issue bonds to raise capital. Companies typically use funds from bonds to improve their businesses in some way. They may open new stores, buy new equipment, or hire more employees with this money. The government also uses bonds for a wide range of purposes. They may put the money towards paving roads, buying new books for libraries, or even military defense.

The amount of money the investor loans the borrower through a bond is called the principal. The borrower agrees to pay back the principal, plus a certain amount of additional money. This extra money is called interest. Both parties agree that the principal and interest will be paid back by a certain date. This is called the bond's maturity date.

You may wonder why big companies and the government issue bonds instead of borrowing money from banks. First, they usually pay a lower interest rate on bonds than they would on a loan to a bank. Second, they can borrow the money for a much longer period of time. Most banks will not lend money at a fixed interest rate for more than five years. A fixed rate stays the same for the life of the loan. Bonds, however, are often issued for as long as thirty or even forty years with a fixed rate.

Companies can also raise money by selling stock. But people who purchase stock are buying a share of the company itself. Stock ownership therefore comes with a certain amount of say in what the company does, plus ownership of a portion of the company's assets and profits. The owners of many companies prefer to keep their companies their own. Bonds don't offer this ownership to investors. They allow companies to borrow the money they need without the owners giving up any control.

By the sixteenth century, bonds were being sold in Italy and the Netherlands. During this time period, the details of the loans weren't always clear. The British solved this problem about two hundred years later when they introduced bonds in the United Kingdom. They made sure that the amount of the bond and its maturity date were clearly stated in the deal. They also made sure that the terms of the bond didn't change within the same issue. An investor could buy a single bond or one hundred (or more) at a time, and the terms would be the same for all of them. This saved time for the investor, and it helped Britain sell more bonds.

Many bonds that have been offered throughout history were issued to help pay for wars. This was also the case for the first bonds sold in

The Beginning of Bonds

King William III of England (1650-1702) established the Bank of England in 1694. When he and his wife, Queen Mary, ascended the throne just five years earlier, the government's money was scarce and its credit was poor. England needed a way to manage both. By issuing bonds, the monarchy was able to pay its war debts—and finance future wars

America. When Britain needed help paying for the Anglo-French War, it passed the bill on to the American colonies. The British government's view was that the war was protecting its colonial citizens, so those citizens should pay for the war. In order to raise funds, the colony of Massachusetts began issuing bonds in 1690. The colony repaid these bonds to investors with money it received from tax payments.

In 1733, a group of Boston merchants decided to issue their own currency. This paper money was also a type of bond. It could be redeemed after ten years for a certain amount of silver. As it happened, the price of silver soon rose by 50 percent due to inflation, making these bonds even more valuable.

Eventually Britain created laws to keep the colonial governments from printing their own money. When this happened, the colonies

Three Pence.

THIS Bill fhall pafs current for *Three Pence*, according to an Act of General Affembly of the Com-mon-Wealth of *Pennfylvania*, paffed the Twentieth Day of *March*, in the Year One Thou-and Seven Hun-ired and Seventy-even. Dated the Tenth Day of *April*, A. D. 1777.

Three Pence.

B

Known best as the printer of the Declaration of Independence, John Dunlap also printed this three-pence note for the Pennsylvania government. Pennsylvania began to issue its own currency in 1723, which was in use until it was replaced by the U.S. dollar in 1793.

began issuing Treasury bills instead. These bonds could be redeemed for gold and silver after two or three years, but they did not serve as currency.

The colonies built up a great deal of debt winning the American Revolution against Britain. They borrowed money from the governments of France and Spain, as well as from private Dutch investors. Following the war, the new government struggled to find a way to repay these debts. Secretary of the Treasury Albert Gallatin decided to buy back bonds that were selling at or below their face value to help repay the money. This created the first open market for bonds in the United States.

Former Senator and Secretary of the Treasury Albert Gallatin disagreed with Andrew Jackson on many issues, including whether the states were responsible for building their own roads and canals.

Gallatin thought that the federal government was responsible for creating roads and canals. Andrew Jackson, however, disagreed. After he became president in 1829, he shifted this responsibility to the states. The biggest problem with the sudden change was that the states lacked both money and experience. In order to finish projects begun by the federal government, the states began issuing bonds. But when it became obvious that not all states could be trusted to repay their loans, many bonds lost their resale value.

INVESTOR TRIVIA

A bond issued by the colony of Massachusetts in 1775 recently appeared on the television show *Pawn Stars*. Issued just after the start of the American Revolution, the bond was printed on a plate made by Paul Revere. Because of its historical value, the bond sold for $12,000.

INVESTOR TRIVIA

The first municipal bond in the United States was issued in New York City in 1812 to build a canal.

The problem only got worse after the Civil War, especially in the South. Ten Southern states defaulted on more than $300 million in principal and interest. They insisted that they were within their rights to refuse to pay the debt based on the US Constitution. The Fourteenth Amendment declares that "neither the United States nor any State shall assume or pay any debt or obligation incurred in aid of insurrection or rebellion against the United States."

Just a year before the start of the Civil War, the national debt of the United States totaled $64.8 million. By the time the war ended in 1865, the national debt had increased to $2.6 billion, more than forty times what it had been in 1860. This debt included $500 million in government-issued bonds.

President Woodrow Wilson signed the Federal Reserve Act into law on December 23, 1913. All national banks were required to join the Federal Reserve System. The biggest goal of this reform was to stabilize the nation's financial systems.

In 1913, the United States created the Federal Reserve System. The main purpose of this central banking system was to regulate US banking and investment policies. President Woodrow Wilson created the Federal Reserve, or the Fed, to make the US economy more stable. The Fed wouldn't just supervise banking. It would also protect the credit rights of consumers, control interest rates, and reduce inflation.

When World War I began, the government decided to issue Liberty bonds to raise money for the war. These government bonds offered investors an interest rate of between 3.5 and 4.5 percent. They sold these new bonds through banks and advertised them as a way to make money and support one's country at the same time.

Over the next century, both government and corporate bonds would undergo many changes. Today, bonds can be a smart part of an investment portfolio. It is important to understand that not all bonds are alike, though. Knowing the differences can help you earn as much interest as possible through these investments. It can also help keep you from losing your hard-earned money.

The US Treasury Building in Washington, DC

The 4-1-1 on
FEDERAL BONDS

If you are interested in buying government bonds, you have many choices. Each type of bond works a little differently. Most are safe investments, but some may work better for you than others. It all depends on how much money you have and when you will redeem the bond with your principal and interest.

You have probably heard the word *Treasuries*. This is the name many people use for the debt securities issued by the US Treasury Department. These investments are sold at auction by the Federal Reserve Bank. One of the biggest differences between the three basic types of Treasuries is the length of time it takes them to reach their maturity dates. Treasury bills take the least amount of time. They mature in a year or less. Treasury notes take between two and ten years to reach maturity. Finally, Treasury bonds mature thirty years from the date they are purchased.

Treasuries offer many benefits to investors. Because they are backed by the US government, most people consider them very safe investments as long as they are kept until their maturity dates. Treasuries are also easy to buy and sell. The longer the term of the Treasury, the more interest you might earn. Longer terms also come with more interest rate risk, though. For example, let's say you buy a thirty-year Treasury bond at 3 percent interest. In three years, you decide you would like to sell the bond, but now rates are at 6 percent. In this case, you might have to sell the bond for less than what you paid for it if you need to get your money out. On the other hand, if interest rates on Treasury bonds drop to 2 percent, you could sell the bond for even more than what you paid for it. Regardless of what happens to interest rates, if you keep the bond until maturity, you will receive all the promised interest plus your full principal.

As long as you keep your Treasury until its maturity date, you won't lose your principal or any of your interest.

When you collect interest from Treasuries, you must report the interest you receive to the Internal Revenue Service, and pay taxes on these earnings.

Although you can purchase Treasuries directly at an online auction through the TreasuryDirect website, most people buy Treasuries through banks, brokerage firms, or as part of other investments like money market funds. They are sold in amounts starting at $100 and go all the way up to $5 million. This wide range makes them a feasible investment for both new and experienced investors. You will have to pay federal income tax on money made through Treasuries, but you won't pay state or local taxes on them.

Treasury bills, or T-bills, mature in four weeks, three months, six months, or one year. These short terms are definitely Treasury bills' biggest advantage. Because they mature so quickly, T-bills carry very little interest rate risk. T-bills can also be purchased on the secondary market. The term may be as short as just a few days in these cases.

Bonds can be for large amounts, such as this 1934 Federal Reserve Certificate bond.

The face value of a Treasury bill is called the par amount. A T-bill is sold for less than its par amount. The difference between the par amount and the price paid is the interest. Par amounts begin at $100 and increase in multiples of $100.

Treasury notes are available for two, three, five, seven, or ten years. Treasury bonds are sold with thirty-year terms. Long-term Treasuries hold the highest interest rate risk. The shorter the term, the less the value will rise or fall in the time before it matures.

INVESTOR TRIVIA

Over 50 million people own US savings bonds.

In addition to Treasury bills, notes, and bonds, the Treasury also offers Treasury Inflation-Protected Securities, or TIPS. These securities are similar to the other Treasuries, but they come with built-in adjustments for inflation. In addition to interest payments, the principal of your investment will also increase with the rate of inflation. TIPS are available in five-, ten-, and thirty-year terms.

The global financial crisis of 2008 had a huge effect on Treasuries. The stock market was down, and large financial institutions were at risk of failing. Many people couldn't afford to pay their mortgages, and some lost their homes to foreclosure. People panicked. Some experts called it the worst economic time in our country's history since the

The financial crisis of 2008 had a devastating effect on investors worldwide. After losing large amounts of money on their investments, many American homeowners couldn't afford to pay their mortgages. This resulted in a record number of foreclosures all over the country.

Great Depression of the 1930s. Many people who owned stock decided to sell it. They feared that they would lose even more money if they held on to their stock instead. Many of them reinvested their stock money in Treasuries. As the number of investors looking for safer investments increased, competition for these securities increased as well. Investors were willing to accept lower interest rates in exchange for safety. Because of the drop in interest rates, the resale values of older, higher-paying bonds rose.

Treasuries are also offered in the form of zero-coupon bonds. The Federal Reserve doesn't sell these investments directly. Investors can purchase zero-coupon bonds from banks or brokers. Investors can buy this type of bond at a deep discount, but the interest that is earned won't be paid until its maturity date. It is very important to understand that you may still have to pay taxes on the interest earned in the years before you redeem a zero-coupon bond. For this reason, the best way to purchase zero-coupon bonds is through an investment such as a college savings plan or an individual retirement account (IRA), which allows you to defer paying taxes on interest.

The last type of Treasury is the US

Some college savings plans allow you to defer or even avoid paying taxes on their earnings.

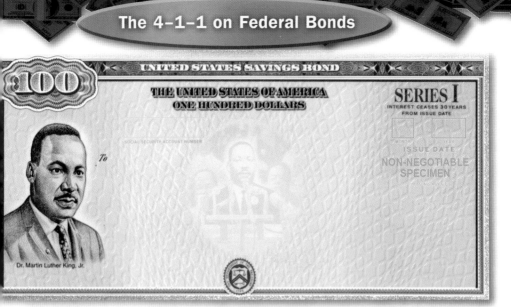

A $100 savings bond is worth $100 from the day you buy it. You must keep it at least twelve months before you redeem it, though.

savings bond. Unlike other Treasuries, these investments cannot be traded. Once you own a savings bond, you only have two choices. You can keep it until it reaches its maturity date, or you can cash it in early. You must own the bond for at least twelve months before cashing it in. In the first five years, cashing in the bond will cause you to lose the last three months' worth of interest that you have earned. You won't lose any of your principal, however. Cashing in a savings bond after five years will only cost you whatever interest it would have earned in later years had you kept it.

At one time, paper savings bonds could be purchased at almost any bank or credit union. Selling savings bonds this way, however, was costing the government a lot of money. In 2002, the Treasury started selling electronic savings bonds through the TreasuryDirect website. Given the choice, most Americans still chose to buy paper bonds. From October 2010 until June 2011, the Treasury sold $1.2 billion worth of savings bonds, but only 11 percent of them were purchased online. The Treasury decided to stop selling paper bonds altogether in 2011. Today these investments can only be purchased electronically through the TreasuryDirect site. The government expects to save $70 million in the first five years by doing away with paper bonds.

Buying bonds online offers investors some benefits as well. First and foremost, electronic bonds cannot be misplaced. Also, electronic bonds are redeemed automatically when they reach their maturity date. All savings bonds that are currently being sold will stop earning interest thirty years after the purchase date. As of July 2011, the Treasury had $16 billion in unredeemed bonds that were no longer earning interest. If you own paper bonds, you can convert them to electronic bonds online.

Today, investors can choose from two types of savings bonds: Series EE and Series I. Each one offers different advantages to investors. Series EE bonds pay a fixed rate. If you want to know exactly how much money you will earn in interest, this is the better savings bond for you. Series I offers an inflation-based interest rate, which changes every six

Both Series EE and Series I savings bonds are extremely safe investments. The biggest difference between the two is that the Series EE bond offers a fixed interest rate, while the Series I bond offers a variable interest rate which changes with the rate of inflation.

Before you buy a bond, be sure to do your homework. You should know all the risks before you purchase any type of investment.

months. With the Series I bond, there is a chance of earning more interest, but there is no guarantee that it will be better than the amount you will earn with a Series EE bond.

Regardless of the series, today savings bonds are sold at face value. This means you will pay $100 for a $100 savings bond. It will then earn interest on top of this principal amount. You can buy savings bonds in any amount you like between $25 and $10,000. In the past, savings bonds were sold for less than their face value. These older bonds earned interest toward their face value instead of on top of it.

INVESTOR TRIVIA

Savings bonds that are redeemed to pay college expenses may be tax exempt. This means that the owner doesn't have to pay taxes on the interest earned. Oddly enough, the interest will only be tax-free if the bond is in a parent's name. As unfair as it might seem, a bond bought in the child's name cannot be granted tax exemption if the child is younger than twenty-four years old.

Did you know that you can help build or expand hospitals by buying certain types of municipal bonds?

CHAPTER 3

Municipal Bonds— TAX-FREE?

Municipal bonds are another type of government investment. Unlike Treasuries, though, these investments are issued by local governments. Cities, counties, and states issue municipal bonds. You can also find municipal bonds that are issued by companies to finance projects that have a public purpose. These include electric utility companies, hospitals, and universities.

Municipal bonds, or "munis," have higher minimum investment amounts than Treasuries. They aren't completely out of reach for a beginning investor, though. Some municipal bonds have minimum investments as low as $1,000 (although many are higher).

Municipal bonds pay lower interest rates than Treasuries, but they do have an overwhelming advantage. You won't have to pay federal taxes on the money you earn through these investments. As long as you live in the state where the bond is issued, they are almost always tax-free on the state and local level as well.

As with so many other investments, 2008 was a very bad year for municipal bonds. Things got better in 2009, but some major changes have occurred since the downturn. Some of the companies that suffered the most in 2008 were municipal bond insurance firms. These companies guaranteed that if the government or company couldn't pay back the bond, then the insurance company would. Unfortunately, many of these companies lost a lot of money during the financial crisis, and some stopped offering the insurance altogether. As a result, very few munis are insured anymore. This makes it even more important to research the finances of the company or government issuing the bond before you buy.

Income tax rates vary from state to state. If you live in a state with high tax rates, you may wonder if tax-free bonds are a better choice for you. Saving on taxes could be an advantage, but sometimes the demand for tax-free munis in high-tax states can be so large that the governments can offer very low interest rates and still sell these bonds. The amount of taxes you pay is based on your annual income. The more money you make, the higher your tax bracket is. If you are in a low tax bracket, you could very well make more money from a high-yield bond that you pay taxes on than from a low-yield bond that

Municipal Bonds—Tax Free?

Bonds that offer tax breaks could help you earn the most money from your investment.

you don't. You will need to compare the safety of the bond, interest rates, and taxes to determine what is the best bond for you.

There are two different types of nontaxable municipal bonds general obligation bonds and revenue bonds. General obligation bonds are issued by state, county, and city governments. The interest paid to investors in general obligation bonds comes mostly from taxes. Revenue bonds can be issued to pay for a particular public project. Airports

The safety of a revenue bond depends on the success of the project. If you buy a bond that helps expand a local airport into an international facility, for example, the company will have the potential of making a lot more money. This money can then be used to pay bond holders their principal and interest.

utilities, hospitals, and toll roads serve the public, but they also make money. This money, or revenue, pays the interest and principal to their municipal bond investors.

General obligation munis are usually considered to be safer than revenue bonds. Because they are backed by the full faith and credit of the government issuing them, even if taxes are not sufficient to pay back a general obligation muni, the government will still repay the bond from other sources. Revenue bonds, on the other hand, do not come with this promise. The issuer only uses revenue from the project to pay back the bond. Because of the higher risk involved, revenue bonds offer higher interest rates.

Revenue bonds are still a relatively safe investment, however. Certainly, it is difficult to predict how a business will do over time, but these projects aren't like other businesses. Revenue bonds are issued to pay for services that everyone needs. We all use electricity and water. We all seek medical care when we get sick or suffer injuries. And many people travel on planes or toll highways every day.

You can keep your risk as low as possible by doing some research before buying a municipal bond. If you are considering a general obligation bond, find out if the city or state usually has a balanced

INVESTOR TRIVIA

Municipal bonds issued by state and local governments have a better bond repayment history than corporations. A municipal bond may be ten to forty times less likely to default than a corporate bond with the same rating.

Low-risk investments might be safe, but they usually offer lower rates of return than investments with more risk.

budget. If it tends to run a deficit, or shortage of funds, you face a higher risk as an investor in general obligation bonds issued by that city or state.

The riskiest revenue bonds are those issued by new organizations and those that are having financial problems. Investing in a utility that hasn't been built yet, for example, can be risky. What if something prevents the project from opening? If you are investing in a toll road, do the present tolls cover all the expenses of keeping up the highway? Any business that is having a hard time paying its bills may not be able to pay its investors either.

INVESTOR TRIVIA

Some bonds are callable bonds. This means that the company or government issuing the bond can repay the bond in full before the maturity date. If this happens, the investor will have to purchase another bond in order to continue earning interest on their principal.

Another way to do your homework about municipal bonds is by researching credit ratings. To understand credit ratings, consider how credit works for people. When a customer applies for a loan from a bank, the loan officer checks the person's credit score. This number tells the bank whether the customer is a good credit risk or not. If he or she has paid back other loans on time in the past, the score will be higher. If the person didn't make payments on time, the score will be lower. Just like people, businesses also have credit ratings, and their bonds have ratings that tell you how much risk they carry. Municipal bonds are rated by independent companies like Moody's and Standard & Poor's using a letter-based credit grading system. The safest municipal bonds are rated AAA. Lower ratings are AA, A, and BBB or BAA. These ratings can be broken down even further—for example, AA1 or AA+ is higher than AA2 or AA, which are higher than AA3 or AA-.

It's not just the credit rating that matters. The history of the rating may also tell you something about the safety of the bond. A bond issued by a utility company might be rated AAA today. If it has dropped to AA or A in the last year, though, it is riskier than an AAA bond that has always had this highest rating.

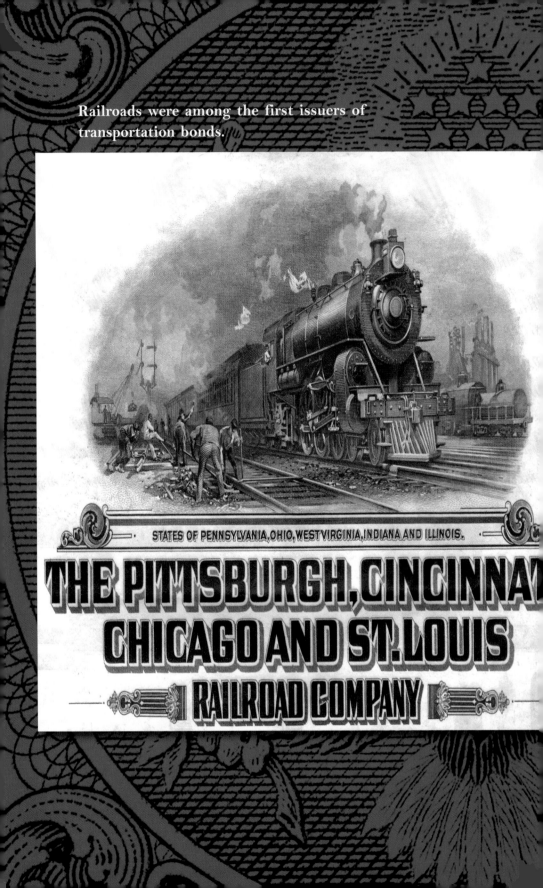

Railroads were among the first issuers of transportation bonds.

STATES OF PENNSYLVANIA, OHIO, WEST VIRGINIA, INDIANA AND ILLINOIS.

THE PITTSBURGH, CINCINNAT
CHICAGO AND ST. LOUIS
RAILROAD COMPANY

The World of
CORPORATE BONDS

Corporate bonds usually fall within one of five categories: financial, industrial, transportation, utilities, and conglomerates. Financial bonds are mainly issued by banks and insurance companies. Industrial bonds are sold by companies that provide goods or services, like technology companies or manufacturing companies. Transportation bonds include bonds issued by airlines and railroads, while companies such as electric and telephone companies issue utility bonds. A conglomerate company does business in two or more of these sectors. Like municipal bonds, new issues of corporate bonds usually start at $1,000.

At one time, bonds issued by utility companies were among the safest bonds investors could buy. After all, nearly everyone needs electricity and a telephone. Most people who lived in an area got their electricity from the same provider. The same was true for telephone service. These companies had monopolies in their markets, because other companies couldn't offer the same service in the same area. This nearly guaranteed that a utility company would prosper.

In the late 1990s, though, deregulation was introduced in numerous states. People wanted to be able to choose their own utility company. They wanted companies to work harder for their business. While this competition was generally a good thing for utility customers, it wasn't a good thing for people who had bought bonds issued by the utility companies. While utility bonds are still considered relatively safe investments, those that do business in deregulated states now carry the same risk as any other company.

Just how risky are corporate bonds? The answer depends on how much homework you do before buying your bonds. Like municipal bonds, the best credit rating for corporate bonds is AAA. From there ratings go down to AA, A, BBB, BB, B, CCC, CC, and C. A rating of BB or lower is said to be below investment grade, or risky. Due to the current state of the economy, very few corporate bonds have a rating of AAA at the moment. An AA rating is still very good, though. Of course, a great credit rating isn't a guarantee. Even big companies that have done well for years go out of business on a regular basis. Investing in corporate bonds is a lot like investing in the stock market. The payoff can be high, but the risk of losing your money also exists.

If you want to buy corporate bonds, here are a few things to consider. Think about the industry. Are most companies in this type of business doing well right now? Where does this company rank in its field? How long has it been in business? How many people have heard

Before buying a corporate bond, research the company as thoroughly as possible. Compare its stock price today to its price one year ago. Also, look for information about the company's performance over the last several years. A stable company that consistently makes a profit is your best bet.

of it? What do you know about the company's management? There is no way to know for sure that the company will be able to pay its bills, but you must be comfortable with your choice.

In addition to the company, consider the bond itself. If a company issues new stock, it will be worth the same amount as any previous stock that the company has sold. If the company issues new bonds, however, the new issue could have very different terms. In general, senior (or older) bonds are safer than junior (or newer) ones. In the event that something goes wrong with the company, senior bonds are paid out before junior bonds.

Some corporate bonds offer investors a higher amount of interest than others. You might assume that these bonds are a better choice, but don't act too quickly. The reason for this bigger reward is that the companies issuing them are more likely to default. These high-yield bonds are frequently referred to as junk bonds. These bonds fall below the investment grade, making them the riskiest of all corporate bonds.

Junk bonds with low ratings can be enticing to new investors. After all, they offer the potential for a big reward. It is important to remember that these bonds carry the highest risk of all corporate bonds, though.

Junk bonds that are rated BB have a better chance of providing you with that high yield than those with a C rating. But keep in mind that the higher the rating, the lower the return will be.

In 2007 and 2008, a large number of investment-grade bonds issued by banks, insurance companies, and airlines fell below investment grade. With the worsening economy, these companies were struggling. Some of the companies ended up recovering from their hard times. Others went out of business.

Predicting which bonds will be a good investment is not an easy task. The best financial advisors in the world cannot guarantee that a particular bond won't default. Even before something bad happens, junk bonds aren't very liquid. This means that they can be difficult to sell if you need your money quickly. If you can sell them, the price will probably be very low. To make matters worse, these investments can drop in value in a very short period of time.

Many financial experts see corporate bonds as something that only experienced investors should buy. If you like the idea of buying corporate bonds, you may want to consider investing in a bond mutual fund instead of buying individual bonds. Investing in individual bonds means taking the time to research each one. It also means a minimum amount for each investment. A bond mutual fund pools the money of many investors and uses it to invest in a broad range of bonds. There are funds specializing in corporate bonds, Treasuries, and even state-specific municipal bonds if you want a fund with local tax benefits. These bonds are managed by financial experts with years of experience. A bond mutual fund usually requires a lower investment and is generally less risky. If one bond in the fund defaults, you won't lose as much money because your investment is spread across many different bonds.

The risk of mutual funds made up of corporate bonds is still high. The value changes based on the economy, interest rates, and of course the value of the individual bonds. You can keep your risk as low as possible by placing your money in a short-term bond mutual fund. Funds made up of bonds that mature in four years or less are best for this purpose. Predicting the direction of interest rates can be almost as tough as predicting which companies will do well in the future.

Whether you are buying investment-grade corporate bonds or junk bonds (or a combination of the two), it is smart to deal with a broker. You will pay a fee to work with a broker, but part of what you are paying for is his or her knowledge and experience. You won't have to pay a fee to a broker if you pick your own bonds, but your risk of losing money will be higher. You could easily lose more money by working on your own than you would pay a broker.

INVESTOR TRIVIA

Exchange-traded funds (ETFs) can include corporate bonds, but they are different from regular mutual funds. ETFs are traded on stock exchanges just like shares of stock.

Before you put your money
in high-risk investments,
make sure the money you are
investing is money that you
can afford to lose.

Risky
BUSINESS

Before you buy your first bond, you must decide if you want to enter the primary market or the secondary market. The primary market offers new issues. These bonds are being sold for the first time. The secondary market deals in bonds that have already been owned by one or more investors.

The primary market is much simpler in many ways than the secondary market. When a company offers a bond, it decides how much to charge for the bond. This is called the offering price. Each investor then pays the same amount for the bond. Municipal bonds can work the same way, but they may also hold auctions to sell their bonds. The investors willing to accept the lowest interest receive the bonds. Simple doesn't mean easy, however. Breaking into the primary market can be very difficult. It helps if you have a working relationship with someone at the bank making the offering for the company. But most small investors don't have the connections to be able to purchase new issues.

Buying bonds on the secondary market is much easier, but it comes with a certain level of risk. It is also much more complicated. You won't be able to make this type of purchase without a broker. It can be difficult to know for sure if the bond you are buying is a good deal, so having a broker you trust is very important. He or she should be knowledgeable about how bonds are priced and how to track them.

Never forget that your broker is making money on the bonds that he or she sells you. When you use a broker, you must pay a commission, or spread. Not all brokers charge fair prices for the bonds they sell, however. For this reason, it is very important that you do your own research. First, you want to find out how much other brokers are charging for this particular bond. Second, you want to compare these prices with what your broker is planning to charge you for the bond. If your broker's price is a lot higher, chances are good that the difference is part of his or her spread.

A great place to find information on corporate and municipal bonds is the Financial Industry Regulatory Authority (FINRA). This agency uses a search engine called TRACE to track the sales of bonds on the secondary market. Brokers are required to report information about corporate bond and municipal bond trades within fifteen minutes of the transactions. You can also visit the FINRA website to find background

INVESTOR TRIVIA

The secondary market has made it possible for smaller investors to buy corporate bonds. Large-scale investors often make money by buying first-issue bonds that smaller investors cannot afford. These buyers sell them to brokers, who break them into smaller amounts before reselling them to numerous small investors.

The Financial Industry Regulatory Authority (FINRA) helps protect American investors by making sure the securities industry operates fairly and honestly. FINRA also works to educate the general public about investing.

information on both individual brokers and brokerage firms. This step can help you make sure you are dealing with a reputable broker.

Another good resource is the Municipal Securities Rulemaking Board (MSRB). The board offers a similar service called the Electronic Municipal Market Access (EMMA). Both FINRA and MSRB provide information to the public free of charge. The language is simple and easy to understand, even if you are new to the investment world. You can also watch a video on the MSRB website that explains what kind of information you will find on the site and how to use it.

If you are new to investing, the secondary market may be more than a little overwhelming. Even more confusing than the secondary market is the international market. In addition to bonds issued by the United States government and American companies, you can buy bonds from other nations' governments, banks, and companies. Learning about buying international bonds can be interesting, but you may want to postpone investing in international markets until you have more experience. Even then, you might decide that you aren't interested in putting your money into international bonds at all.

The first thing you should know about international bonds is that they aren't always sold in foreign currency. The United States has the largest bond market in the entire world. For this reason, many foreign governments and companies sell their bonds in US dollars. You may also find international bonds sold in euros (the currency of France, Germany, Italy, and many other European countries), in yen (the currency of Japan), or other types of currency.

A foreign bond is a specific type of international bond that is issued by a company or government in one country and sold to investors in a second country. For example, an international bond from a Japanese company is a foreign bond if it is sold here in the United States to American investors in US dollars. (Here we call this type of bond a Yankee bond.) At the same time, a bond from an American company that is sold in Japan to Japanese investors in yen is also a foreign bond.

Even if you completely understand the process of buying international bonds, extreme caution should be used in this area. One of the reasons to be especially careful is that it can be hard to know exactly how stable a particular country is. Greece provides a good

INVESTOR TRIVIA

People who buy bonds issued by foreign countries in foreign currency need to remember that exchange rates are always changing. This means that an investor could make more by purchasing an international bond, or they could make less—depending on how the value of the other currency changes in relation to the value of the US dollar.

The country of Greece is still in the midst of a dire financial crisis. Because the country took on more debt than it could pay back, many investors (in Greece and elsewhere) than both the interest and the principal on the bonds they bought from the Greek government.

example of the problems you could face by investing in international bonds.

Beginning in 2010, Greece faced one of the worst debt crises in history. For years, the country had been adding up debt that it couldn't afford to pay back. As of 2013, Greece owed numerous other nations large amounts of money, unemployment was at a record high, and the government couldn't agree on what to do about the situation. Anyone who has purchased bonds issued by the country is very unlikely to receive the interest or the principal. If a solution isn't found soon, the unpaid debt could also place other countries in a bad economic position. The crisis could have a domino effect throughout Europe.

If you want to make as much money as you can from bonds without much risk, the best thing you can do is something called laddering. This strategy for buying bonds is much simpler than it sounds. Laddering simply means buying numerous bonds that will mature at different times. A single bond will pay you a certain amount of interest. Several smaller bonds will pay you different rates. Some may pay less,

One of the best ways to lessen your overall risk is by buying numerous smaller bonds that will mature at different times. This strategy is called laddering.

and some may pay more than others. Your overall chance of earning more money is greater with laddering, though.

Another benefit to laddering is that it keeps more of your money liquid. If you need cash, you will be able to redeem a smaller bond without losing as much interest. This can be very helpful if an unexpected expense arises. Over time, laddering also allows you to move your money into other investments more gradually if you decide to go that route. After all, bonds are just one of the many options available to investors today.

Investment Firms that Specialize in Bonds

Alamo Capital
1-877-68-ALAMO (1-877-682-5266)
http://www.alamocapital.com/
Locations in California, Nevada, Arizona, Illinois, and Michigan

Eaton Vance Investment Managers
Two International Place
Boston, MA 02110
1-800-225-6265
http://corporate.eatonvance.com/index.php

Envision Capital Management, Inc.
11755 Wilshire Blvd, Suite 1140
Los Angeles, California 90025
1-800-400-0989
http://www.envisioncap.com/index.php

The GMS Group
New Jersey, New York, Connecticut:
1-800-453-6230
Florida: 1-800-453-6231
Texas: 1-800-453-6234
http://www.gmsgroup.com/

GW&K Investment Management
222 Berkeley Street
Boston, MA 02116
1-800-225-4236
http://www.gwkinvest.com/

HJ Sims
1-800-457-1935
http://www.hjsims.com/
Locations in Connecticut, Florida, New Jersey, Minnesota, Texas, and Maryland

David Lerner Associates, Inc.
1-877-367-5960
http://www.davidlerner.com/
Locations in New York, New Jersey, Connecticut, and Florida

Secure Vest Financial Group
1-800-MY-BONDS (1-800-692-6637)
http://www.securevest.com/faq.html
Locations in New Jersey and Florida

Stoever Glass & Co.
30 Wall Street
New York, NY 10005
1-800-223-3881
http://www.stoeverglass.com/

Many people think of bonds as very safe investments. In some cases this is true. Savings bonds, for example, are among the safest investments a person can make. Other types of bonds, however, carry certain risks, including interest rate risk and credit risk. Ideally, you want to buy bonds that offer the highest possible interest at the lowest possible price. It is also important that the issuer has a good track record of honoring debt securities.

Bonds that investors purchase on the secondary market can be especially risky, since their prices move according to the yield. Bonds that offer higher interest rates will go up in price if interest rates fall. Likewise, bonds that offer lower interest rates will go down in price if rates go up. You must also consider the price you will pay a broker for bonds. The trick to making the most from bonds is buying at the right time and from a broker who offers reasonable fees.

Bamford, Janet. *Street Wise: A Guide for Teen Investors.* Princeton, New Jersey: Bloomberg Press, 2000.

Gardner, David, Tom Gardner, and Selena Maranjian. *The Motley Fool Investment Guide For Teens.* New York: Fireside, 2002.

Karlitz, Gail. *Growing Money: A Complete Investing Guide for Kids.* New York: Price Stern Sloan, 2010.

Kristof, Kathy. *Investing 101.* New York: Bloomberg Press, 2008.

On the Internet

FINRA: "Investors"
    http://www.finra.org/Investors/index.htm
Municipal Securities Rulemaking Board: "Investor Toolkit Video"
    http://www.msrb.org/Investor%20Toolkit%20Video.aspx
TreasuryDirect: "Treasury Securities & Programs"
    http://www.treasurydirect.gov/indiv/products/products.htm

US Treasury building

CNN Money. "Investing in Bonds." *Money 101.* http://money.cnn.com/magazines/moneymag/money101/lesson7/index.htm

Fahey, Jonathan. "Electric Deregulation Finally Takes Off." *Forbes,* April 12, 2010. http://www.forbes.com/forbes/2010/0412/outfront-electricity-deregulation-constellation-power-moves.html

"How Greece Has Got Itself in This Mess." *The Telegraph,* June 17, 2012. http://www.telegraph.co.uk/finance/financialcrisis/9334170/How-Greece-has-got-itself-in-this-mess.html

Krantz, Matt. *Investing Online for Dummies.* Hoboken, New Jersey: Wiley Publishing, Inc., 2010.

Richelson, Hildy, and Stan Richelson. *The Money-Making Guide to Bonds.* Princeton, New Jersey: Bloomberg Press, 2002.

Thau, Annette. *The Bond Book.* New York: McGraw Hill, 2011.

TreasuryDirect. "Treasury Securities & Programs." http://www.treasurydirect.gov/indiv/products/products.htm

Wild, Russell. *Bond Investing for Dummies.* Hoboken, New Jersey: Wiley Publishing, Inc., 2007.

broker (BROH-ker): a person or company that buys and sells investments on behalf of another person or company in exchange for a commission

capital (KAP-i-tuhl): cash or other assets owned by a business

commission (kuh-MISH-uhn): a sum of money paid to a sales agent or broker for his or her services

default (dih-FAWLT): a failure to meet an obligation, such as repayment of a debt

defer (dih-FUR): to postpone or delay until a certain time in the future

deficit (DEF-uh-sit): a state in which spending exceeds income

deregulation (DEE-reg-yuh-ley-shuhn): the act of reducing the government's power in a particular industry

foreclosure (fawr-KLOH-zher): the act of taking away property due to nonpayment on a loan

inflation (in-FLEY-shuhn): a rise in the general level of prices of goods that leads to a decrease in the value of money

interest (IN-ter-ist): a sum paid or charged for borrowing money

high-yield (HAHY YEELD): paying a higher yield or annual interest rate than most other investments of the same type

liquid (LIK-wid): in cash or easily convertible into cash

maturity date (muh-CHOOR-i-tee deyt): the date on which a bond or loan is due to be repaid to the investor

monopoly (muh-NOP-uh-lee): a business that is the only business offering a particular product or service in a market

principal (PRIN-suh-puhl): the original amount of money placed in an investment before interest or profit is earned

tax bracket (TAKS BRAK-it): the rate at which a person is taxed based on his or her income

tax exempt (TAKS ig-ZEMPT): not subject to taxes

About the
AUTHOR

Tammy Gagne has authored more than seventy-five books for both adults and children over the last decade. She has been investing for twice this time. In addition to managing her own portfolio, she has taught her teenage son about the details of his investments, enabling him to make some of his own decisions in this area. She believes that young people should know how money works, so their money can work for them instead of vice versa. When young people understand investing and feel in control of their finances, they get excited money. They also tend to have more of it.